The Paul Mellon Bequest

TREASURES OF A LIFETIME

INTRODUCTION BY

John Baskett

CATALOGUE BY

Malcolm Warner

YALE CENTER FOR BRITISH ART · 2001

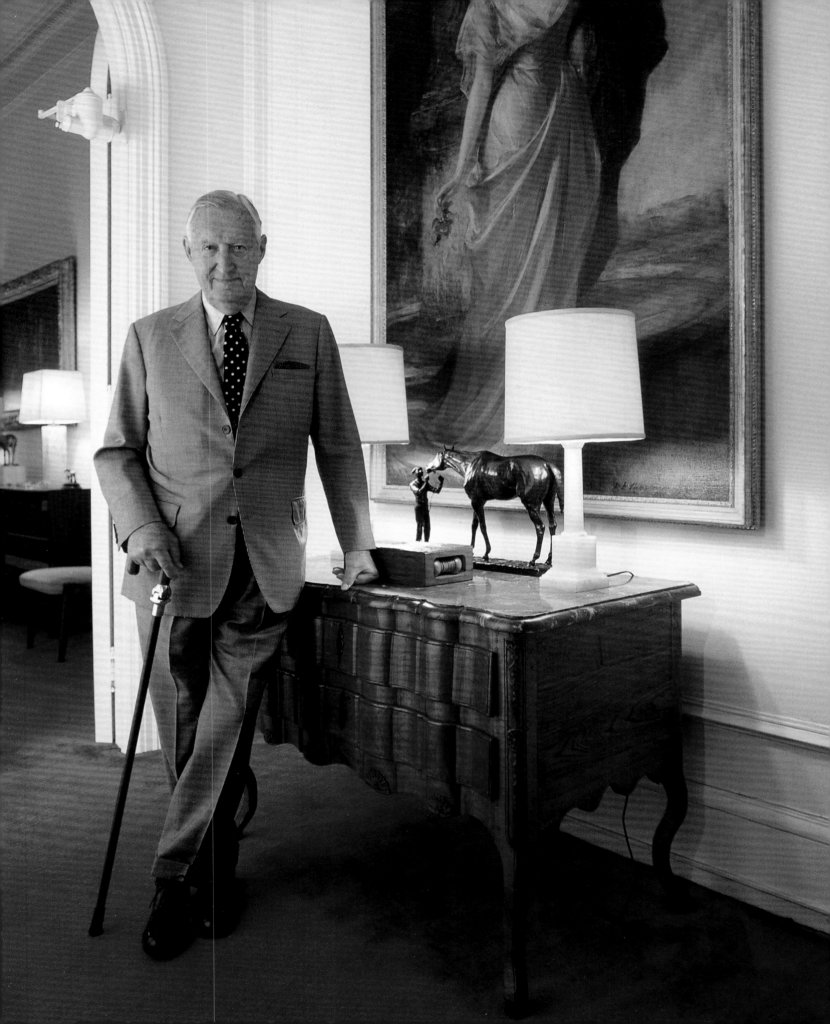

Published on the occasion of the exhibition
The Paul Mellon Bequest: Treasures of a Lifetime
Yale Center for British Art, February 17–April 29, 2001

Photography by Richard Caspole except as follows:
Jonathan Becker, page 3
Joseph Szaszfai, pages 16–17
Steve Tucker, pages 15, 18

Design by Greer Allen
Color separations by Professional Graphics
Binding by Mueller Trade Bindery
Printed by Thames Printing Company

Front cover:
ROBERT BURNARD
John Gubbins Newton and his sister, Mary Newton,
c. 1833: detail (see page 61)

Frontispiece:
Paul Mellon at his office,
Park Avenue, New York, 1992

Back cover:
JOHN SELL COTMAN
Horse loaded with artist's paraphernalia, c.1835–40
Pencil, 9 3/8 x 12 5/8 in.
Reference: Egerton and Snelgrove 1978, 28

Contents

JOHN CONSTABLE

Somerset House Terrace from Waterloo Bridge, c.1819

Oil on panel, 6 1/8 x 7 3/8 in.
References: Taylor 1964, 20 (no. 65);
Reynolds 1984, 40–1 (no. 19.37)

Foreword

Paul Mellon was a lover of art and knowledge, nature and the environment, horses and the sport of horses. His life was dedicated to acts of exceptional philanthropy and personal generosity for the widest public benefit. He was Class of '29 and Yale's greatest donor and benefactor.

When Paul Mellon pledged in 1966 his collection of British art, together with a building to house it and an endowment to sustain it, he created an institution of national and international significance within the structure of Yale. When the British Art Center opened in 1977, the collection had grown to become the finest and most comprehensive representation of a national school of art ever created beyond the shores of that nation.

Paul Mellon's final bequest to Yale is of a scale and generosity unparalleled in the 300 years of the University's history. Over 300 paintings and sculptures, over 1.000 drawings and prints, 5,000 rare books, and an endowment so substantial that it will enable the British Art Center to operate in perpetuity, enabling it to add significantly to its historic collection of British art. The generosity extends beyond the walls of the British Art Center, to the Yale University Art Gallery and to the central endowments and educational mission of the University as a whole.

The exhibition, *The Paul Mellon Bequest: Treasures of a Lifetime*, initiates a year long celebration of Yale's most steadfast friend. How appropriate that this celebration should form the centerpiece of Yale's tercentenary year, when the University looks forward to the next millennium and traces its proud history of scholarship, learning and public service.

The final bequest of works of art, rare books, personal memorabilia and sustaining endowment, sets the capstone on this institution. For the bequest contains those works of art Paul Mellon loved first and longest, throughout his productive life. First amongst equals is the gift of George Stubbs's *Pumpkin and a stable-lad* which was the first oil painting Paul Mellon acquired. Although Paul Mellon in his lifetime had given the Yale Center for British Art sixteen paintings by Stubbs, his final bequest would add a further eleven, thus giving Yale the largest, most refined and most comprehensive representation of this quintessential English genius.

Paul Mellon's love of British sporting art was an open, self-declared passion. He believed that a serious injustice had been done to the achievements of British sporting artists and sought to rectify it by his avid but discriminating collecting of Ben Marshall and James Ward, J. F. Herring and John Ferneley, Alfred Munnings and Robert Bevan, John Skeaping and Tessa Pullan. The finest works of these artists he kept as a personal collection and which is now shown *in extenso* to the public for the first time.

The celebration of Paul Mellon's gift is rooted in a profound sense of gratitude—at once institutional and personal. He enriched his beloved University with an art museum of matchless beauty. Paul Mellon gave to his generation an experience of beauty, stimulus, delight and lasting pleasure, and now that is given in perpetuity to succeeding generations.

PATRICK MCCAUGHEY
Director

Acknowledgments

For their help and advice on the introductory essay, John Baskett would like to thank Brian Allen, Beverly Carter, and Duncan Robinson. In the notes on individual works in the exhibition, Malcolm Warner depended a great deal on Judy Egerton's invaluable catalogue of Paul Mellon's sporting and animal paintings. Norma Lytton helped with research on some of the works in the exhibition, Dorcas MacClintock with advice on equine matters, Lorian Peralta-Ramos with information on the paintings by Alfred Munnings, and John Taylor with information on the artist Robert Burnard, his great-great-grandfather.

As always, Beverly Carter was helpful in every possible way, from the enormous task of moving the works in the bequest from Upperville and New York to the Center, to details such as providing photographs of the Brick House and Paul Mellon's study in the New York house. The Center owes her and the staff of the Brick House, Michelle Tompkins, Carolyn Colbert, Linda Cook, and Eugene Howard, a huge debt of gratitude for their efficiency and professionalism.

M. W.

ROBERT BEVAN

Aldwych, 1924

Oil on canvas, 24 1/2 x 32 in.

AUGUSTUS WALL CALLCOTT

Windsor from Eton, c. 1808–9

Oil on canvas, 29 1/2 x 44 1/4 in.
Possibly exhibited at the Royal Academy,
London, 1809

Paul Mellon was christened in St George's Chapel, Windsor Castle, and spent some of the happiest days of his childhood on summer visits to Windsor: "From those distant summers I remember huge dark trees in rolling parks, herds of small friendly deer, flotillas of white swans on the Thames, dappled tan cows in soft green fields, the grey mass of Windsor Castle towering in the distance against a background of huge golden summer clouds; soldiers in scarlet and bright metal, drums and bugles, troops of grey horses; laughing ladies in white with gay parasols, men in impeccable white flannels and striped blazers, and always behind them and behind everything the grass was green, green, green . . . There seemed to be a tranquility in those days that has never again been found, and a quietness as detached from life as the memory itself." [1] *He hung Callcott's painting in a place of high honor, over the fireplace in his study in New York (see page 18).*

1. *A Collector Recollects* 1963, in Yale Center for British Art 1977, vi.

Introduction *by John Baskett*

There can be little doubt that Paul Mellon was the greatest collector of the second half of the twentieth century and, in the whole field of British paintings, drawings, books and prints, he may well have been the greatest collector of all time. His incomparable gifts and bequests to the Yale Center for British Art comprise 1,600 paintings and over 130 sculptures, 18,000 drawings and watercolours, 21,000 prints, and 27,000 books. The Paul Mellon Collection bears three distinctive characteristics. With certain exceptions, it confines itself roughly to the period stretching from the ministries of Robert Walpole in the early eighteenth century to the accession of Queen Victoria in 1837; it contains a large number of sporting works and, perhaps most striking, it was formed on a truly monumental scale.

Paul Mellon always directed his interests towards areas where he had personal experience of life, and the time he spent at university, both in the United States and later in England, had a particularly powerful effect on him. Like many young people at that stage in their lives, his mind was very receptive to outside influences, while the future appeared to stretch out before him as vast uncharted territory. He arrived at Yale in 1925 at the age of eighteen and, over the following four years, the lectures he heard, delivered by such legendary figures as William Lyon Phelps, Chauncey Tinker and Bob French, filled him with an appetite for English literature. The reading habit stayed with him throughout his long life and, from an early stage, he found himself drawn towards an interest in the eighteenth century. Once, when inscribing a copy of Wilmarth Lewis's Horace Walpole lectures to me, he wrote: "To John, who spends part of his life in the eighteenth century, as I do…" The sheer vitality of the period appealed to him. His reading profited on account of his suffering from insomnia for, although he had no difficulty in

getting to sleep, he would often wake up about three o'clock in the morning and then fill in the time until dawn by opening a book. Over the years, with his retentive memory, he became extremely well read.

When he had taken a good degree at Yale in 1929, Paul Mellon went on to Cambridge, which he described as his "next educational venture."[1] After Yale's tightly disciplined and structured system of lectures, followed by discussions with questions and answers, he found the *laissez-faire* atmosphere of Cambridge at that period was not particularly conducive to study. He recalled that the relaxed approach to teaching prompted a postcard from his tutor, a Mr. Gascoigne, with the message, "Dear Mr. Mellon, would you kindly let me know what you will be doing next term?"[2]

Mr. Mellon rowed for Clare College, and it was during this period that he discovered foxhunting, a sport that he took up in earnest with Chunky Hatfield, an American friend and undergraduate at Corpus Christi College. As a result, Cambridge provided him with a sporting, rather than an academic, education. This budding passion for the horse lasted a lifetime and led Mr. Mellon to a variety of equestrian pursuits, including point-to-pointing, trail riding, racehorse ownership, and the establishment of a renowned breeding operation. As he pointed out later, "I rode constantly, I rowed intermittently, I read a little."[3] The sporting life he had been leading, incidentally, induced in him considerable anxiety when his father, then United States Ambassador to the Court of St. James, arrived in Cambridge to watch him receive his degree. His two years at Clare College, however, furthered his romantic love affair with England, and it was also the time when he started collecting books, particularly color-plate books and books on racing and hunting. The book

---

1. *A Collector Recollects* 1963, in Yale Center for British Art 1977, vi.
2. *Reflections* 1992, 119.
3. *A Collector Recollects* 1963, in Yale Center for British Art 1977, vii.

J. M. W. TURNER

*Clare Hall
and King's College Chapel,
Cambridge, from the banks
of the River Cam,* 1793

Pencil and watercolor
7 13/16 x 10 3/4 in.

collecting was to flourish over a broad field, and the depth and importance of the collection he formed has only lately become more widely known through his bequests and through William Reese's recent Malkin Lecture at the University of Virginia.

When, thirty years later and in his fifties, Paul Mellon began to collect pictures and drawings, it was quite natural that he should incline towards the period to which he had been drawn by his literary studies, and that sporting art should play a significant part. Mr. Mellon's

collecting of British art really got under way in 1959 when he met Basil Taylor, the art historian. Both men shared an interest in the then little-appreciated eighteenth-century animal painter, George Stubbs. Taylor was making a special study of the artist and Paul Mellon had many years earlier bought a particularly beautiful example of Stubbs's work, *Pumpkin with a stable-lad.* Taylor felt a mission to rehabilitate the reputation of British painting in its native country. Having met with a largely negative response in the English academic world, he encouraged Mr. Mellon to form a

ALFRED MUNNINGS

Paul Mellon on Dublin, 1932–3

Oil on canvas, 31 x 37 1/2 in.

"He pulled a bit and was strong as a locomotive," Paul Mellon wrote of his Irish hunter Dublin, "but although a so-called three-quarter-bred, he had enough foot and staying power not to disgrace me in several point-to-points. He could have jumped the Eiffel Tower. I think it was Dublin more than anything else who assured my lifelong addiction to hunting. He had huge quarters and a wonderful long front, and his eye had the 'look of eagles.'"[1] Munnings painted the portrait largely during Paul Mellon's visit to England in 1932, the horse at its stables in Gloucestershire and Paul Mellon in the studio in Chelsea. Before delivering the finished work, Munnings sent a photograph. Paul Mellon wrote to him that he found the bushy willow tree on the left a little disturbing and asked whether he could do something to make it less prominent. "Sometime later I got a blast back saying in the first place, the tree wasn't a willow, it was a pollarded oak, and second, he had no intention of changing anything whatsoever. So that was that."[2]

1. *Reflections* 1992, 228.
2. Ibid., 229.

collection of British art in the United States. As a result of their discussion, Mr. Mellon engaged Basil Taylor as his advisor—at Taylor's insistence an unpaid position. All this was decided over coffee at Claridge's Hotel in London, but decisions taken seemingly casually are often arrived at from longstanding, unconscious motives.

Whether either party really foresaw the momentous outcome from this meeting will never be known, but in no time at all it became clear that the collection was going to overflow any domestic bounds. In fact, the grander scheme, which may have been envisaged from the start, emerged, and collecting continued, in the knowledge that the end game would result in a museum, with everything being placed in the public domain. Obviously, as someone whose time was at a premium, Mr. Mellon needed advice, but this didn't mean that he wished to delegate decisions over making acquisitions, and these decisions remained his then and throughout his life. As he always said, "I like to keep my finger on the button."

He considered the golden era of his collecting to have been during the sixties. At that time the art trade was relatively innocent and unspoiled. There had been World War II, and older dealers, remembering the recession of the thirties, were grateful for what they got. There was far more material available on the market, and business was done quietly. He grew increasingly ill at ease with the investment mentality and the aggressive display of wealth that later became the characteristics of the salerooms.

Not long after Paul Mellon had begun collecting in earnest, he established in London a foundation to publish work and forward interest in British art. This Paul Mellon Foundation for British Art had Basil Taylor for its first director. Mr. Mellon later endowed its successor, the Paul Mellon Centre for Studies in British Art, and this Centre now publishes art books in collaboration with Yale University Press and acts as the London wing of the Yale Center for British Art.

Mr. Mellon always felt that education held a key to the good life. Shortly after graduating, he had considered a career in teaching but also had in mind the suggestion made to him by a fellow student that he should use his inheritance to be a philanthropist. He realised that he could forward his educational aims far more effectively through philanthropy than by working as a college professor. What better, then, than to provide Yale with these "windows" onto eighteenth-century and early nineteenth-century life? He once told me that if just one student were to look at his collection and subsequently find his life changed for the better by it, he would be satisfied. One of Mr. Mellon's most endearing qualities was this concern for others.

When Mr. Mellon gave the greater part of his collection of British art to the Center in the 1970s, he was careful to retain a large portion of the sporting pictures for his own enjoyment, along with a selection of other favourites that were of a non-sporting nature. His several houses were decorated predominantly with French and American paintings collected jointly by Paul Mellon and by "Bunny," his wife, but he reserved for himself two locations where the picture hang was almost exclusively English. The first, on his Virginia estate of some four thousand acres, modestly described as "the farm," was the Brick House, designed for Paul Mellon and his first wife, Mary, by William Adams Delano in the style of the eighteenth-century Hammond-Harwood house in Annapolis, Maryland and completed in 1941. When he was no longer living there, Mr. Mellon had the Brick House converted into a picture gallery and library to house his growing collections. This conversion was completed in 1961.

After the main body of pictures left for Yale in 1977, Mr. Mellon devoted the wall space in the Brick House exclusively to sporting paintings. As you entered the door you were greeted, among other pictures, by James Ward's *John Levett hunting at Wychnor, Staffordshire,* John Ferneley's *Archery meeting in Bradgate Park, Leicestershire,* and the intriguing full-length painting of *John Gubbins Newton and his sister, Mary Newton,* the attribution of

The Brick House, Upperville, Virginia

The Brick House: Main Hall

Brick Hall

Living Room

The Study,
Paul Mellon's house
on East 70th Street,
New York

which puzzled everyone until a signature recently revealed the artist to be a little known painter named Robert Burnard. Walking through the Brick Hall with its Stubbs paintings of *Pumpkin with a stable-lad* and *Lustre, held by a groom,* and the same artist's painting on earthenware, *Labourers,* of 1781, one reached the "Old Library" where Mr. Mellon's Americana and Virginiana material was shelved. Next to that was a little room that had held the vellum-bound library of John Locke, the English seventeenth-century philosopher, purchased in 1959 and later given to the Bodleian Library at Oxford, and on the second floor there was the large library that had been used for the J. R. Abbey Collection of British color-plate books before most of the volumes were given to the Yale Center. The Trophy Room, also located on the second floor, held the many trophies for thoroughbred racing won by Mr. Mellon's horses in the United States and in England, and the Degas Room, to a design by his wife, housed a large number of wax sculptures by Edgar Degas, including the enchanting statue of the *Little Dancer of Fourteen*

Years. This treasure trove was within easy walking distance of his family residence, Oak Spring. Paul Mellon could stroll over with his dog whenever he felt like it and spend as much time as possible enjoying many of the works of art included in the present exhibition.

The second *schatzkammer* was to be found in Mr. Mellon's study in the New York house. In this small room, with its low ceiling, it was a delight to find oneself on a winter's evening, seated with Paul Mellon in comfortable chairs near an open log fire, beside a table bearing prawn canapés and martinis, and engaging in the sort of relaxed conversation at which he was so adept. One's gaze would wander towards the large E. W. Cooke painting of a sailing boat calmly passing "the Needles" off the Isle of Wight. Books were everywhere, neatly stacked or on shelves, and there was ordered clutter on his large desk. The fireplace wall was covered with little Constable sketches and behind one's head rested the tiny Stubbs enamel of a sleeping leopard and Blake's little tempera painting of *The Horse.*

Mr. Mellon's taste for small pictures was well known, believing as he did that they were frequently more intimate than the large, studied composition. He certainly felt that Constable's small oil sketches conveyed a wonderfully immediate approach to nature, and he found great pleasure getting them framed and hanging them close together on the wall. He kept a hammer and nails within easy reach for this work, which he described as "a mild form of occupational therapy."[1]

Paul Mellon's diffident charm and exemplary good manners captivated all those who knew him. These characteristics were allied to a gentle, self-deprecating humor. The fact that he could see the ludicrous side of situations often went a long way towards allaying the anxieties of others. He was always reluctant to recognise his own importance. Shortly before his death he told me that all life ends in failure, certainly of the body, and sometimes of the mind, too. Happily, he never experienced the latter. After death, he said he expected to become just a little speck in a vast universe and that no one would remember him in a hundred years' time. He did, however, claim that the one certainty in his mind was that he had had a wonderful life, and that nothing could destroy that. He added, too, that he thought he had left his affairs in good order. This last remark struck me as an astonishing understatement. Apart from the happy memories he left with family and friends, there were the large number of munificent bequests, among them the generous benefactions to the National Gallery of Art, particularly of French pictures collected jointly by him and his wife, to the Virginia Museum of Fine Arts, to his old school and his old universities and, above all, to that jewel in his crown, the Yale Center for British Art.

I think, given the personal basis of the exhibition, it would be appropriate to close with some excerpts from

1. *Reflections* 1992, 282.

Mr. Mellon's memoir, *Reflections in a Silver Spoon*, in which he expressed in his own words his reasons for collecting:

"My interest in British art is part of my fascination with British life and history. From childhood and from Cambridge days I acquired a fondness for the English landscape and for the ever-changing light…I grew to love English country life and country sports. I became a lifelong devotee of foxhunting and racing. All these interests converged to make me ready to collect paintings, drawings, books, and prints, wherever the subject matter is related to English life in the eighteenth and early nineteenth centuries . . .

I am so often asked, 'What makes you want to own one work of art more than another?' I think I have always had a keen visual sense (unlike most people I dream mostly in colors). One of the reasons I've always liked riding, foxhunting, racing or just walking around in the beauty of the countryside – green fields, bright autumn leaves, sunsets, rainbows, high wedges of flying geese and their eerie honking, cattle grazing, cattle lowing in the distance – is that these scenes long remain vivid in my mind's eye. It is an inner picture gallery that I can return to in quiet moments . . .

When I buy a painting, some feature about it may remind me consciously or unconsciously of some past event, thought, feeling, moment of pleasure or even of sadness. It might be a fortuitous combination of colors, or a certain calmness, or a beautiful sense of proportion. In the case of a portrait, perhaps it is the sitter's character, air of intelligence, or a hint of humor. Would I like her or him? It seems to me that art makes one feel the essence of something, turning the ordinary, everyday object or scene into a universal one. Like poetry for Wordsworth, it is 'emotion recollected in tranquillity' . . .

I think I can truthfully say that I have not collected in order to hoard, and I hope the pleasure I have derived from my collecting activity is shared by those who now visit the National Gallery, the Yale Center for British Art, and the Virginia Museum of Fine Arts."[1]

1. *Reflections* 1992, 276, 293–4, 294, 296.

WILLIAM BLAKE
The Horse, c.1805
Tempera, with pen and black ink,
on a copper engraving plate, 4 3/16 x 2 1/2 in.
Ref: Taylor 1963, 200 (no. 382);
Egerton, 1978, 152–4 (no. 148)

Blake made this small painting from one of his illustrations to William Hayley's BALLADS, FOUNDED ON ANECDOTES RELATING TO ANIMALS, *published in 1805. Hayley was a minor poet and biographer now remembered chiefly as Blake's patron. His ballad "The Horse" tells of the courage of a mother who stands between her child and a runaway horse, which she tames by looking it fixedly in the eye.*

Catalogue

by Malcolm Warner

English Country Life

"From 1907 until 1914, from my first year to my seventh, my parents spent almost every summer in England, and my sister and I were invariably taken with them. I suppose it was in those summers that I first developed a taste for the English countryside, for English houses, English rivers, English parks, English skies, English clouds . . . at this great distance it all melts into a sunny and imperturbable English summer landscape."

— Paul Mellon, 1963[1]

The vision of English country life that emerges from the Paul Mellon bequest is a subtly changing one. It shows artists broadening their horizons, moving beyond the aristocratic park and garden and into the fields and villages, drawn by the beauties and pleasures of simple nature. We can trace this Romantic feeling for the countryside from James Ward's *The Reapers* (page 27), to its high point in the work of John Constable, and on to the paintings of Robert Bevan and Alfred Munnings in the early twentieth century.

Paul Mellon particularly enjoyed Constable's oil sketches. He believed the breezy freshness and changeable light that were so much part of his idea of England to be better captured in small, spirited sketches than in larger works of high finish. "My own feeling is that size has nothing to do with the quality or the importance of a work of art," he remarked, "just as preliminary drawings or sketches in oil or pastel often have an immediacy and an emotional appeal far greater than the final canvas. Among many other examples I could cite are Constable's small oil sketches, which appeal to me equally with his larger paintings, and his techniques and mastery of the brush are as formidable in them as in his masterpieces. In the spring of 1991 I saw the comprehensive Constable exhibition at the Tate Gallery in London, and I am now even more convinced that small is beautiful."[2]

By the time of his death Paul Mellon had already given some thirty of Constable's oil sketches to the Yale Center for British Art. Of the fifteen Constables in his bequest, all are small works and a dozen are sketches. He hung most of them in the densely packed display of small paintings and works on paper in the study of his house in New York (see page 18).

1. *A Collector Recollects* 1963, in Yale Center for British Art 1977, v–vi.
2. *Reflections* 1992, 271–2.

CHARLES PHILIPS

*The Watson-Wentworth
and Finch Families*, c.1731–2

Oil on canvas, 29 1/2 x 49 in.
Reference: Taylor 1963, 115 (no. 218)

The man on the right of the group wearing the Order of the Bath is Thomas Watson-Wentworth, Baron Malton, later 1st Marquis of Rockingham; the woman seated near the center is his wife, Mary Finch, and the rest of the party consists of their five children, a nurse, three of the baroness's sisters and two of her brothers. Thanks to Baron Malton's influence as a powerful landowner, both of his brothers-in-law sat as Whig members of parliament. At the time of the portrait he was engaged in rebuilding his country house, the colossal Wentworth Woodhouse in Yorkshire.

THOMAS HUDSON

Portrait of a young woman
of the Fortescue family of Devon,
probably 1740s

Oil on canvas, 50 x 40 in.

HENRY WALTON

Elizabeth Bridgman,
sister of the artist, c.1771–5

Oil on canvas, 13 5/8 x 11 5/8 in.
References: Taylor 1963, 137 (no. 261);
Egerton 1978, 136–7 (no. 130)

THOMAS GOOCH

Marcia Pitt and her brother George Pitt,
later 2nd Baron Rivers, riding
in the park at Stratfield Saye House,
Hampshire, 1782

Oil on canvas, 27 1/8 x 25 1/8 in.
Exhibited at the Royal Academy, London, 1783
References: Taylor 1964, 67 (no. 242);
Egerton 1978, 147–8 (no. 141)

JAMES WARD

The Reapers, 1800

Oil on canvas, 18 1/8 x 24 1/4 in.
Reference: Egerton 1978, 211 (no. 223)

JAMES WARD

Gloucestershire Old Spot,
c.1800–1805

Oil on panel, 11 3/4 x 15 in.
Reference: Egerton 1978, 212 (no. 225)

JOHN CONSTABLE

East Bergholt Church, 1809

Oil on paper laid on panel
7 15/16 x 6 3/16 in.
Reference: Reynolds 1996, 135 (no. 09.39)

Among the highlights of Paul Mellon's bequest is a group of early oil sketches by Constable, painted in and around the artist's home village of East Bergholt, Suffolk. The young Constable's favorite subjects were village landmarks such as the parish church and East Bergholt House—his family home and birthplace—and everyday sights in the valley of the river Stour, where his father Golding Constable owned watermills. Sketching in oils outdoors, in front of the motifs, he tried to see the world afresh and create a more natural form of landscape painting.

JOHN CONSTABLE

Golding Constable's riding-horse, c.1810

Oil on panel, 14 x 18 1/4 in.
References: Egerton 1978, 232 (no. 250);
Reynolds 1996, 153 (no. 10.54)

JOHN CONSTABLE

East Bergholt House, c.1809

Oil on canvas, 5 3/4 x 10 in.
Reference: Reynolds 1996, 149 (no. 10.30)

JOHN CONSTABLE

Barge below Flatford Lock, c.1810

Oil on canvas, 7 11/16 x 12 1/4 in.
Reference: Reynolds 1996, 150 (no. 10.37)

JOHN CONSTABLE

Flatford Mill, c.1810–11

Oil on panel, 6 1/2 x 11 3/4 in.
References: Taylor 1963, 76 (no. 99);
Reynolds 1996, 162 (no. 11.41)

JOHN CONSTABLE

Flatford Mill, c.1810–11

Oil on panel, 6 5/16 x 11 9/16
Reference: Reynolds 1996, 162 (no. 11.42)

JOHN CONSTABLE

Flatford Lock, c.1810–11

Oil on paper laid on canvas
14 1/2 x 14 1/2 in.
Reference: Reynolds 1996, 167 (no. 12.10)

One of the mills on the river Stour owned by Constable's father was at Flatford, and the buildings, waterways, and locks at the mill were to provide some of the recurrent motifs of Constable's art. This is one of a series of on-the-spot oil sketches that he used as raw material for the larger, more finished studio-picture FLATFORD MILL FROM THE LOCK, *shown at the Royal Academy exhibition of 1812; in the larger work the view extends further to the left to include the distinctive red-brick buildings of the mill.*

JAMES WARD

Grey Arabian stallion,
the property of Sir Watkin Williams-Wynn, c.1815–20

Oil on canvas, 39 x 49 in.
Reference: Egerton 1978, 218 (no. 233)

JACQUES-LAURENT AGASSE

Study of a fox, c.1810–20

Oil on panel, 6 1/4 x 8 1/2 in.
Reference: Egerton 1978, 186 (no. 193)

JACQUES-LAURENT AGASSE

*Studies of a fox, a barn owl, a peahen,
and the head of a young man,* c.1810–20

Oil on canvas, 9 1/2 x 18 5/8 in.
Reference: Egerton 1978, 187 (no. 194)

JOHN CONSTABLE

Osmington Village, 1816—17

Oil on canvas, 10 1/8 x 12 in.
Reference: Reynolds 1996, 226 (no. 16.58)

The village of Osmington in Dorset, about five miles east of Weymouth, was the home of Constable's closest friend, the clergyman John Fisher. In 1816 the artist and his new wife Maria stayed with Fisher at his vicarage for much of their honeymoon, and he based this painting on a sketchbook drawing he made at that time. The vicarage is the grey building to the left with smoke rising from its chimney. Constable gave the work to Fisher and his wife along with pendant portraits of them both.

JOHN CONSTABLE

Hampstead Heath, c.1822

Oil on canvas, 10 5/8 x 12 5/8 in.
Reference: Reynolds 1984, 110–11 (no. 22.49)

JOHN CONSTABLE

Hadleigh Castle, 1828–9

Oil on board, 7 7/8 x 9 7/16 in.
Reference: Reynolds 1984, 201 (no. 29.3)

This is a preparatory sketch for the grandest of the Constables already in the collection of the Yale Center for British Art, HADLEIGH CASTLE, THE MOUTH OF THE THAMES— MORNING AFTER A STORMY NIGHT, *given by Paul Mellon as part of his inaugural gift in 1977. Constable first visited Hadleigh Castle, on the northern shore of the Thames estuary, in 1814. He made a rough pencil sketch of the place at that time, but it was not until fourteen years later, looking for a scene that expressed his feelings on the recent death of his wife, that he decided to work up the composition as a large exhibition picture. The present sketch seems to have been his first elaboration upon the drawing, from which he went on to a sketch on the same scale as the final work; the latter is now in the Tate Collection, London. He showed the final work at the Royal Academy exhibition of 1829.*

JOHN CONSTABLE

Sir Richard Steele's Cottage, Hampstead,
c.1831—2

Oil on canvas, 8 1/4 x 11 1/4 in.
Possibly exhibited at the Royal Academy,
London, 1832
References: Taylor 1963, 84 (no. 114);
Reynolds 1984, 235 (no. 32.6)

*Constable lived in the village of Hampstead, north of London, from
1821 until his death in 1837. This work shows the view from
Hampstead Road (now Haverstock Hill), with the dome of St. Paul's
Cathedral in the distance and Sir Richard Steele's Cottage on the right.
The cottage was known as such because the famous early eighteenth-
century essayist lived there for a time, largely to escape his creditors
in London.*

a

b

DEAN WOLSTENHOLME, JR.

Studies of carrier pigeons, 1837
a. Red pied carrier
b. Grizzle carrier

Oil on canvas, each 14 1/8 x 12 in.
Reference: Egerton 1978, 314–15 (no. 341)

JAMES INSKIPP

Study of poppies, 1832

Oil and pencil on board, 16 x 9 in.
Reference: Reynolds 1984, 243
(no. 32.48, attributed to Constable)

EDWIN LANDSEER

Favourites, the property
of H. R. H. Prince George
of Cambridge, 1834–5

Oil on canvas, 40 x 49 1/2 in.
Exhibited at the Royal Academy, London, 1835

Prince George of Cambridge, aged fifteen or sixteen at the time of this painting, was a first cousin of the future Queen Victoria. The prince's pony, dogs, and falcons seem to await his arrival from the door on the left, presumably to go out hawking in the royal park at Windsor; through the door is a distant view of Windsor Castle. Landseer painted black-and-white Newfoundland dogs like Prince George's so ably and often that the variety became known as the "Landseer," a name still in common use. Despite his skill in painting animals, Landseer was not a favorite artist of Paul Mellon, who disliked his sentimentality and anthropomorphism; in this case the mitigating circumstance was probably the setting at Windsor, a place dear to him from his childhood.

THOMAS THORNYCROFT

Queen Victoria on horseback, 1853

Published by the Art Union of London, 1854
Bronze, height 21 1/4 in.

JOSEPH EDGAR BOEHM

Girl on horseback, with boy and dog, 1865

Bronze, height 16 in.

JOHN FERNELEY

Archery meeting in Bradgate Park, Leicestershire, 1850

Oil on canvas, 46 1/2 x 99 in.
References: Taylor 1963, 154 (no. 293);
Egerton, 1978, 250–1 (no. 271)

Archery was a fashionable pursuit for both men and women in early Victorian England, and the meeting depicted is probably that of a local club for enthusiasts. Bradgate House in Leicestershire was a ruin, and its surrounding parkland was open for such public recreations. Ferneley lived a few miles away at Melton Mowbray. He seems to have painted this work as a genre subject, without portraits of particular individuals and without a commission. He never sold it, and it was still in his possession at his death in 1860.

EDWARD WILLIAM COOKE

*Opposite my house
at Barnes,* 1862

Oil on panel,
11 15/16 x 18 15/16 in.

ALFRED MUNNINGS

*Epsom Downs—
City and Suburban Day:
The Last of the Gypoes,*
c.1921

Watercolor, heightened
with bodycolor,
14 1/2 x 21 in.

ALFRED MUNNINGS

On the Downs, c.1920

Oil on canvas, 30 x 36 1/4 in.
Exhibited at the Royal Academy, London, 1933

ROBERT BEVAN

The Caller at the Mill, c.1918–19

Oil on canvas, 22 x 26 in.
Reference: Bevan 1965 (no. 68)

From 1912 until his death in 1925, Robert Bevan regularly spent his summers in Devon. He painted THE FORD *and* THE CALLER AT THE MILL *while staying at an isolated and barely furnished cottage called Lytchett, on Hart's Farm, in the Blackdown Hills. Both recall the stylized landscapes painted by Gauguin and other avant-garde French artists at Pont-Aven in Brittany, where Bevan spent formative periods of his early career.*

ROBERT BEVAN

The Ford, 1918

Oil on canvas, 22 x 26 in.

Hunting, Shooting, Fishing

"Hunting is another example of the reaction which has set up inside me against business, the city, modern industrial drabness, the suppression of the natural emotions and feelings . . . It involves the use of the horse, that instinctive animal, and man's mastery of the horse . . . It requires physical skill, good judgement, quick thinking, and the age-old thrill of the chase and the kill . . . There is nothing mechanical about it. It is natural, as old as the hills, literally."

—Paul Mellon, 1936 [1]

Of the works of art that Paul Mellon kept for his own pleasure until his death, the majority dealt with the great passions of his life as an outdoorsman, foxhunting and horseracing. The quotation above is from what he called a memorandum to himself, written at the age of twenty-nine, in which he tried to set down what meant most to him in life and why he must resist the business career his father was encouraging him to pursue. For him business and industry meant the unnatural, the ugly, the inhibited; hunting and racing were part of the world of nature, beauty, and feeling that he wished to embrace. On the one side was modern society; on the other were older ways of life, England, and— he felt— his own true self.

He first rode to hounds when he was a student at Cambridge and continued in both England and the States until he was seventy years old; from 1954 to 1959 he was Joint Master of the Piedmont Hunt near his home in Virginia. It was also at Cambridge that he began to collect prints and books dealing with sporting subjects. His enjoyment of the chase was to be inseparable from his enjoyment of sporting art and literature, and he relished works of sporting comedy, especially the novels of R. S. Surtees. In later life, with modest humor, he would compare himself to Surtees's popular character Mr. Jorrocks, a Cockney grocer devoted to sport. "I have grown to look on myself more and more as an anachronism, an incongruity, a sort of latter-day Jorrocks," he wrote toward the end of his autobiography, "an emissary of the past . . . innocent of the great complexities of the day." [2]

During his lifetime, most of the paintings of hunting, shooting, and fishing scenes in Paul Mellon's bequest hung in the Brick House on his estate in Virginia. Together they bear witness to the rise of field sports in the eighteenth and early nineteenth centuries, and the developing idea of the English sporting gentleman. In James Ward's portrait of John Levett hunting (page 57), for instance, we see the combination of naturalness and masculinity that was so much part of the Englishman's identity at the time. They also show the sporting life opening up, becoming less the preserve of rich landowners and more available to middle-class and city-dwelling enthusiasts such as Mr. Jorrocks.

1. Quoted in *Reflections* 1992, 152.   2. *Reflections* 1992, 392.

THOMAS SPENCER

Scipio, a spotted hunter, the property of Colonel Roche, 1753

Oil on canvas, 39 x 52 3/4 in.

Reference: Egerton 1978, 54–5 (no. 56)

ARTHUR DEVIS

John Orde, his wife Anne,
and his eldest son William, c.1754–6

Oil on canvas, 37 x 37 7/8 in.
References: Taylor 1963, 118 (no. 223);
Egerton 1978, 59–60 (no. 60);
D'Oench 1980, 60 (no. 31)

The Orde family lived in Morpeth, Northumberland. Here the young
William Orde returns from shooting and presents his stepmother and
father with a pheasant; the father has before him what appears to be a
legal document. At the same moment a black servant arrives with a letter.
The choice of these events as the basis of the portrait may have had some
particular family significance that has been lost.

GEORGE STUBBS
Studies of foxhounds, c.1760

Oil on paper laid on board,
each 5 3/4 x 8 3/4 in.

JOHN WOOTTON
Releasing the hounds, c.1740–50

Oil on canvas, 18 1/2 x 40 in.

JAMES DUNTHORNE

*John Sidey and his hounds
at a farmhouse near Hadleigh,
Suffolk,* 1765

Oil on canvas, 35 1/2 x 54 in.
Reference: Egerton, 1978, 111 (no. 107)

*According to a label on the back of the frame, this painting records an
actual incident from a day's foxhunting, when hounds pursued a fox onto
the roof of a farmhouse. The work was commissioned by John Sidey of
Pudneys Farm, Bures Hamlet, Essex, who appears on the right, riding a
grey horse; the hounds were probably his private pack. The artist, James
Dunthorne, was a provincial portraitist based in nearby Colchester.*

HENRY WALTON

Portrait of a sportsman, possibly Robert Rayner, c.1770

Oil on canvas, 41 x 33 1/2 in.

References: Taylor 1964, 67 (no. 245); Egerton 1978, 135–6 (no. 129)

GEORGE STUBBS

Greenland falcon, 1780

Oil on panel, 32 x 39 in.
References: Taylor 1963, 169
(no. 321); Egerton 1978,
91–2 (no. 89)

GEORGE STUBBS

*Brown and white Norfolk
or Water Spaniel*, 1778

Oil on panel, 31 3/4 x 38 1/4 in.
References: Taylor 1963, 171 (no. 326);
Egerton 1978, 91 (no. 88);
Egerton 1984, 140 (no. 101)

*The Norfolk Spaniel, which no longer
exists as a pure breed, was used by
sportsmen to spring and retrieve game
from water. Stubbs presents the animal
as the slightly melancholy hero of its
own watery world, looming like a giant
over river banks, water plants,
and weeping willow.*

GEORGE MORLAND

A Party Angling and
The Angler's Repast,
c.1785–9

Oil on canvas, each 25 x 30 in.
Reference: Egerton 1978,
169–70 (no. 167)

BENJAMIN WEST

Gentlemen fishing, 1794

Oil on slate, 12 1/8 x 17 in.
Exhibited at the Royal Academy, London, 1795
Reference: Von Erffa and Staley 1986, 417 (no. 446)

The gentlemen are fishing on Dagenham Breach, a lake formed by a breach in the river-wall on the north bank of the Thames a few miles below Greenwich; the shipping in the background on the left is river traffic. According to an account of the painting by Benjamin West's sons, the party includes the artist himself and his friend Sir Hugh Palliser, governor of Greenwich Hospital. The faces are not rendered in detail, but West is probably identifiable as the man in shirtsleeves elegantly handing a fish to a servant, and Palliser as the older man seated on the far left of the group. In its everyday subject the work was unusual for West, who painted largely in a grand, classical idiom. When it was shown at the Royal Academy, a critic remarked that it showed more talent in a few square inches "than is to be found in as many acres of his painted statues!"

PHILIP REINAGLE
Spearing the Otter,
1805

Oil on canvas,
14 1/2 x 20 1/4 in.
Reference: Egerton 1978
144–5 (no. 136)

GEORGE MORLAND
Pheasant shooting
c.1790

Oil on canvas,
15 7/8 x 20 1/2 in.

JAMES WARD

*John Levett hunting at Wychnor,
Staffordshire*, 1817

Oil on canvas, 39 1/4 x 51 1/4 in.
Possibly exhibited at the Royal Academy,
London, 1818

*The Levett family of Staffordshire were on close terms with Ward, and
bought and commissioned a number of works from him. Here John
Levett has climbed a hill high above the rest of the hunt, where he cuts
a heroic and commanding figure, the mud spattered on his coat serving
as a reminder of the hard riding he has done. Only he and his hunter
can see the fox, which is running over the hill on the right. The view of
the Trent valley in the background shows the artist's close study of the
landscapes of Rubens.*

HENRY ALKEN

Duck shooting in winter, c.1820–30

Oil on canvas, 8 3/4 x 11 in.
Reference: Egerton 1978, 252 (no. 274)

BEN MARSHALL

Portrait of a sportsman,
possibly Richard Prince,
c.1821–5

Oil on canvas, 40 x 34 in.
References: Taylor 1963,
151 (no. 287); Egerton 1978,
204–7 (no. 218); Noakes 1978,
50 (no. 181)

< *Left*
HENRY ALKEN

Pheasant shooting,
c.1820–30

Oil on canvas, 8 3/4 x 11 in.
Reference: Egerton 1978,
252 (no. 273 [1])

< *Right*
HENRY ALKEN

Partridge shooting,
c.1820–30

Oil on panel, 9 x 11 in.
Reference: Egerton 1978,
252 (no. 273 [2])

When Paul Mellon bought this painting, it was misidentified as a self-portrait. The main
evidence against the idea is the sportsman's gun: it is a tube-lock percussion gun datable to
after 1820; Ben Marshall was over fifty years old by this time, whereas the face in the
portrait is clearly that of a younger man. In 1975 Judy Egerton discovered an engraving of
a detail of the painting—the pointer holding a partridge in his mouth—in the SPORTING
MAGAZINE *of October 1825. The magazine identified the pointer as Damon, who once*
belonged to the rakish Colonel Henry Mellish, a racehorse owner and gambler, and lived
with Mellish's trainer at Newmarket, Richard Prince. Mellish died in 1817, and in any
case bore no resemblance to the sportsman in the portrait. Prince, on the other hand, was
alive and still only in his twenties when the portrait was painted. He may well have kept
Mellish's dog, and Egerton's suggestion that the portrait may be of him is highly plausible.
Ben Marshall lived at Newmarket himself, and would certainly have known Prince, whose
grandfather and father of the same name had also been trainers there.

JACQUES-LAURENT AGASSE

Groom mounted on a hunter,
holding another by the reins,
c.1805

Oil on canvas, 23 3/4 x 29 3/4 in.

JOHN FERNELEY

Bay hunter, 1828

Oil on canvas, 28 x 36 in.
Reference: Egerton 1978, 242 (no. 263)

ROBERT BURNARD

John Gubbins Newton and his sister, Mary Newton, c.1833

Oil on canvas, 92 1/2 x 56 1/2 in.
References: Taylor 1963, 149 (no. 283);
Egerton, 1978, 284–9 (no. 309)

The children were the only son and daughter of John Newton and his wife Charity Gubbins, who lived at Millaton House in Devon. With its strange, almost naive appearance— the awkward poses, the blocky modeling in the faces and clothing, the meticulous attention to detail in passages such as the hair— the portrait is difficult to place within early nineteenth-century British portraiture. When Paul Mellon bought it from the dealer Jeremy Maas in 1961, it was attributed to Jacques-Laurent Agasse, the Swiss animal painter who worked in England. In 1978 Judy Egerton argued for a reattribution on stylistic grounds to the Scottish artist John Zephaniah Bell. The present attribution to Robert Burnard was established in a recent cleaning, when the inscription "R. Burnard pinxit" was discovered near the upper left corner. Burnard was a provincial portraitist who was born in Cornwall in 1800 and presumably worked mainly in south-western England; in 1840 he emigrated to Adelaide, Australia.

a

b

JOHN FREDERICK HERRING, SR.

The Suffolk Hunt, 1833
Oil on canvas, each approx. 11 x 15 in.

a. Going to Cover near Herringswell
b. Gone Away

c

d

c. Full Cry
d. The Death

THOMAS WOODWARD

Grey shooting pony,
probably the property
of Johnston King,
with a groom, 1835

Oil on canvas, 17 x 21 in.
Reference: Egerton 1978,
321 (no. 351)

JOHN FERNELEY

Edward Horner Reynard
and his brother George
grouse-shooting
at Middlesmoor, Yorkshire,
with their gamekeeper
Tully Lamb, 1836

Oil on canvas,
34 1/4 x 42 1/8 in.
Reference: Egerton 1978,
247–8 (no. 268)

JOHN FERNELEY

Foxhunting scenes, painted on
Lord Edward Thynne's snuff box, 1832–3

Oil on gold, height 1 1/2 in.; diameter 3 3/8 in.
Reference: Egerton 1978, 247 (no. 267)

HENRY CALVERT

Thomas Cholmondeley, 1ˢᵗ Lord Delamere, on his hunter
(study for "The Cheshire Hunt at Tatton Park"), 1839

Oil on panel, 16 x 12 in.

ANSON AMBROSE MARTIN

James Taylor Wray
of the Bedale Hunt,
with his dun hunter, c.1840

Oil on canvas, 20 5/8 x 25 in.
Reference: Egerton 1978, 338–9 (no. 372)

a

b

HENRY ALKEN

Hunting scenes, c.1840
Oil on canvas, each approx.
18 x 24 1/4 in.

a. The Meet

b. Drawing the Cover

c. In Full Cry

d. The Kill

c

d

Alken was a prolific draughtsman, engraver, and painter of sporting subjects whose work often takes serial form. Some of his prints were published under the pseudonym "Ben Tally-Ho!" He rode to hounds himself, and spent much time in the English mecca of foxhunting, Melton Mowbray in Leicestershire. In all likelihood the present series shows episodes from a hunt in that part of the country.

JOHN DALBY

Beagles in full cry, 1845

Oil on canvas,
14 1/2 x 19 1/4 in.
Reference: Egerton 1978,
312 (no. 338)

WILLIAM BARRAUD

*Couple of foxhounds, the property
of Lord Henry Bentinck,
with a Jack Russell terrier,* c.1845

Oil on canvas, 44 x 56 in.
Reference: Egerton 1978, 335–6 (no. 369)

ADRIAN JONES
"Gone Away," c.1887
Bronze, height 19 1/2 in.

JOHN FREDERICK HERRING, JR.
Returning from the hunt,
c.1860s

Oil on canvas,
20 1/2 x 26 in.

ROBERT BEVAN

Found, c.1896

Pencil, crayon, and wash,
9 7/8 x 13 1/4 in.

ROBERT BEVAN

The Flying Pack, c.1896

Pencil and crayon,
9 3/4 x 13 in.

JOSEPH CRAWHALL

"The Master." Hark to Statesman, c.1900

Watercolor and bodycolor, 21 x 17 in.

"SNAFFLES" (CHARLES JOHNSON PAYNE)
*The Bullfinch: "Black as yer hat on this side
and glorious uncertainty on the other,"* c.1913
Charcoal, watercolor, and bodycolor, 14 7/8 x 21 3/4 in.

ALFRED MUNNINGS

The French Pack at the Entrée des Ecuries,
Château de Chantilly, 1921

Oil on canvas, 32 x 25 1/2 in.

Racing

"There are the same elements in racing that attract me as in hunting, although it is more its aesthetic quality . . . It is the colour, the movement, the speed, the excitement, the competition, the skill of riding, the cleverness of the horses, and the primitive element of luck . . . But it is mostly the love of the horse, the well-kept, well-trained, beautifully moving horse, the horse as an object of art."

Paul Mellon, 1936 [1]

Paul Mellon fell in love with horseracing, like foxhunting, when he was a student at Cambridge. He saw his first races at nearby Newmarket, and that remained his favorite course throughout his life. He bought his first racehorse in 1933 and his first painting of a racehorse, George Stubbs's *Pumpkin with a stable-lad* (page 81), three years later. In the postwar years he raised his activities as an owner-breeder to a more serious level and began to concentrate on flat racing. The highlight of his life in racing was the career of the famous Mill Reef in the early 1970s, "those halcyon days when Mill Reef won the Gimcrack, the Derby, the Eclipse, the King George and Queen Elizabeth stakes, as well as that icing on the cake, the Arc de Triomphe at Longchamp." [2] Bred by Paul Mellon at his Rokeby Farms, Mill Reef was one of the great classic racehorses of all time.

In Paul Mellon's imagination the thoroughbred was an archetype, representing nature and the forces of life itself. The high symbolic response to the horse that he once described in some remarks on Stubbs was as much his own as the artist's: "I think he saw in the horse, in his alertness and muscularity, a way of representing life itself in all its movement, form, vitality, colour, strife and mystery. His horses are alive and beautiful because they were in his soul; he saw them as symbols of many life forces rather than as mere conveyances, necessities, implements. Just as his paintings of lions, tigers, zebras, cheetahs and other wild animals glow with vibrant power, so his horses give off an aura of grace, transforming the perils of energy and wildness into a controlled sense of tense expectation." [3]

The racing paintings in Paul Mellon's bequest tell a similar story to the hunting paintings, that of a relatively closed, aristocratic recreation broadening and becoming less exclusive: the establishment of classic races such as the Derby, first run in 1780, changed the race meeting from a small local affair into an important public event. All the major painters of turf subjects are richly represented in the bequest, from James Seymour to George Stubbs, Ben Marshall and James Ward, and into the twentieth century with Alfred Munnings. The greatest of these was without doubt Stubbs, Paul Mellon's favorite artist, whose works he collected devotedly. The bequest contains no less than eleven paintings by Stubbs, bringing the total number in the Center's collection to twenty-seven.

1. Quoted in *Reflections* 1992, 152.   2. Baskett 1980, foreword, 7.   3. Ibid.

JAMES SEYMOUR

Bay racehorse with jockey up,
c.1730

Oil on canvas, 12 x 14 in.

JAMES SEYMOUR

*The Stables
and Two Famous
Running Horses
belonging to His Grace
the Duke of Bolton,* 1747

Oil on canvas, 24 1/2 x 29 1/4 in.
References: Taylor 1963, 163 (no. 311);
Egerton 1978, 46–7 (no. 50)

JAMES SEYMOUR

The Duke of Devonshire's
Flying Childers, 1742

Oil on canvas, 40 x 50 in.
Reference: Egerton 1978, 45–6 (no. 49)

Foaled in 1715, the great Flying Childers was bred by Colonel Leonard
Childers at Doncaster and bought from him by the Duke of Devonshire
as a yearling. He never lost a race, and is now recognized as the first
supreme thoroughbred racehorse. The demand for portraits of him
continued long after his career was over and Seymour painted a number
of variations on the present work, most of them dated in the 1740s.
The groom steadying him with the reins wears the Duke of Devonshire's
livery of blue and buff.

GEORGE STUBBS

Newmarket Heath,
with a rubbing-down house, c.1765

Oil on canvas, 12 x 16 in.
References: Taylor 1963, 167 (no. 318);
Taylor 1971, 208 (no. 33); Egerton 1978,
77–8 (no. 76); Egerton 1984, 82–3 (no. 53)

Rubbing-down houses were storerooms for grooming equipment, at which stable-lads would rub horses down with cloths and straw after races or exercises. The present work is one of a pair of studies of the same rubbing-down house from different viewpoints; the other is now in the Tate Collection, London. Stubbs seems to have made them in preparation for the backgrounds to portraits of the famous horse Gimcrack, although he clearly used them again in other racehorse portraits with a Newmarket setting. "Not only are they delightful in themselves, extremely rare as examples of the painter and a clue to his method of working," wrote Basil Taylor in a letter to Paul Mellon of 2 January 1961, "but I know no English landscapes quite like them in their naturalism before the lifetime of Constable." [1]

1. Yale Center for British Art.

GEORGE STUBBS

Lustre, held by a groom, c.1760–2

Oil on canvas, 40 1/8 x 50 in.
References: Egerton 1978, 68 (no. 68);
Egerton 1984, 68 (no. 40)

Lustre, foaled in 1754, by Blank, was owned first by the Duke of Ancaster and later by Frederick St. John, 2nd Viscount Bolingbroke, for whom he raced successfully at Newmarket in 1760–1. Known to his friends as "Bully," Bolingbroke was a famous figure in the world of racing, both as an owner and as a gambler. He was one of Stubbs's most important early patrons, and commissioned LUSTRE *and at least seven other racehorse portraits from him. Comparing this work to* THE DUKE OF DEVONSHIRE'S FLYING CHILDERS *by James Seymour (page 77), we see how Stubbs breathed life and beauty into the prosaic tradition of British equine portraiture. His anatomically informed description of a horse's stance and musculature went together with an impeccable feeling for design. There was nothing new about the profile view in portraits of horses, but in Stubbs's hands it took on the order and refinement of classical relief sculpture.*

WILLIAM CRAFT, after OZIAS HUMPHRY

George Stubbs, c.1777

Enamel on copper, 6 3/4 x 5 3/4 in.
Reference: Egerton 1984, 26 (under no. 2)

GEORGE STUBBS

Pumpkin with a stable-lad, 1774

Oil on panel, 32 3/8 x 39 7/8 in.
References: Taylor 1960, 32 (no. 20);
Taylor 1963, 168 (no. 319); Taylor 1971,
210 (no. 66); Egerton 1978, 87 (no. 84)

Pumpkin, by Matchem out of Old Squirt Mare, won a number of races at Newmarket in the years 1772 to 1775. His owner was Thomas Foley, later 1ˢᵗ Baron Foley, who commissioned Stubbs's portrait. This was the first painting Paul Mellon purchased, long before he began collecting seriously and on a large scale. He and his first wife Mary bought it from Knoedler's in London in 1936. "We both were bowled over by the charming horse, the young boy in a cherry-colored jacket, and the beautiful landscape background," he later recalled. "The price was five thousand dollars, and I bought it immediately. It was my very first purchase of a painting and could be said to be the impetus toward my later, some might say gluttonous, forays into the sporting art field." [1] *With its suggestions of morning, green freshness, and the friendship between a boy and a horse, the work went to the heart of the vision of England that Paul Mellon formed in his own boyhood. It remained his favorite British painting throughout his life.*

1. *Reflections* 1992, 280–1.

GEORGE GARRARD

Portrait of a racehorse, possibly Disguise,
the property of the Duke of Hamilton, with jockey up, 1786

Oil on canvas, 33 1/2 x 42 1/2 in.

References: Taylor 1963, 179 (no. 343); Egerton 1978, 161–3 (no. 158)

BEN MARSHALL

John Hilton, Judge of the Course at Newmarket;
John Fuller, Clerk of the Course; and John Stevens,
a trainer, probably 1804

Oil on canvas, 19 1/4 x 15 1/4 in.
References: Egerton 1978, 196–7 (no. 207);
Noakes 1978, 46 (no. 147)

BEN MARSHALL

The jockey Frank Buckle, the owner-breeder
John Wastell, his trainer Robert Robson,
and a stable-lad, probably 1802

Oil on canvas, 18 1/4 x 14 5/8 in.
References: Egerton 1978, 194–5 (no. 205);
Noakes 1978, 34 (no. 52)

BEN MARSHALL

Muly Moloch being rubbed down at Newmarket, 1803

Oil on canvas, 39 7/8 x 50 in.
Reference: Noakes 1978, 37 (no. 79)

A chestnut colt by John Bull out of Mistletoe, Muly Moloch was foaled in 1798; after some wins he was beaten in a race at Newmarket in 1805 and quit the turf. The "Muly" part of his name presumably came from "mule," and "Moloch" from the ancient god who demanded human sacrifices; this hints at a mean streak, which is borne out by his uncooperative demeanor in the portrait. He was bred and owned by the Earl of Darlington, who almost certainly commissioned the work. The men engaged in a discussion on the left are all Darlington's employees: Trotter, a farmer; Hardy, his trainer; and Thompson, a gardener. Paul Mellon had MULY MOLOCH *set into a panel above the living-room mantelpiece at the Brick House; the same room contained the other Ben Marshalls in his collection and a portrait of the artist by his son Lambert (page 85).*

BEN MARSHALL

Broodmare with foal
and a terrier, 1822

Oil on canvas, 40 x 50 in.
References: Egerton 1978,
202 (no. 215); Noakes 1978,
48 (no. 163)

LAMBERT MARSHALL

Ben Marshall, c.1825

Oil on canvas, 14 x 12 in.

HENRY BERNARD CHALON

*Quiz, after his last race
at Newmarket,* 1807

Oil on canvas, 30 1/2 x 43 3/4 in.

The inscription on the frame provides a detailed account of Quiz's *ancestry, his
successive owners, the races he won, and the horses he beat. By Buzzard out of
Miss West, he was foaled in 1798; among his ancestors were the famous
Matchem and Flying Childers (see page 77). In 1801 he won the St. Leger
Stakes at Doncaster, one of the horses he beat being his contemporary Muly
Moloch (see page 84). Most of his victories were at Newmarket. After winning a
race in the first Spring Meeting there in 1807 he was retired to the stud of his
then owner, Lord Rous.*

HENRY BERNARD CHALON

The Clarence Gold Cup at Hampton, 1815

Oil, on a four-fold mahogany screen, overall 70 x 94 in.
Reference: Egerton 1978, 225 (no. 242)

GEORGE GARRARD

Turk, a greyhound, the property of George Lane Fox, 1822

Oil on panel, 11 3/4 x 14 in.

Reference: Egerton 1978, 166 (no. 165 [1])

a

JAMES POLLARD

Epsom Races, 1834–5

Oil on canvas, each approx.
12 1/8 x 18 5/8 in.
References: Selway 1972,
35 (nos. 194–5, 197–8);
Egerton 1978, 274–5 (no. 299)

a. The Betting Post

These scenes of a race meeting at Epsom in Surrey, where the English Derby is run, are from a series of six published in the form of aquatint prints in 1836. The whereabouts of the other two, SADDLING IN THE WARREN *and* THE GRAND STAND, *are at present unknown. From the first scene,* THE BETTING POST, *Pollard places some emphasis on the gambling that accompanied the races. In the final painting he changes the setting from Epsom to Tattersall's, near Hyde Park Corner in London. It was on the premises of this celebrated horse auctioneers that betting accounts would be settled and disputes adjudicated on the Monday following the races.*

b

c

d

JAMES POLLARD

Epsom Races, 1834–5

Oil on canvas, each approx.
12 1/8 x 18 5/8 in.
References: Selway 1972,
35 (nos. 194–5, 197–8);
Egerton 1978, 274–5 (no. 299)

b. Preparing to Start
c. The Race Over
d. Settling Day at Tattersall's

a

b

HENRY ALKEN

Scenes from a steeplechase, c.1840–50
Oil on canvas, each 10 x 14 in.
Reference: Egerton 1978, 254 (no. 277)

a. Taking a hedge
b. Another hedge

c

d

c. Near the finish
d. The winner

BENJAMIN HERRING

Silks and Satins of the Turf, 1865

Oil on panel, 20 x 43 1/2 in.
Reference: Egerton 1978, 347–8 (no. 381)

JOHN FREDERICK
HERRING, SR.

Steeplechase cracks:
Allen McDonough
on Brunette, Tom Oliver
on Discount,
and Jem Mason on Lottery,
c.1846

Oil on canvas (unfinished),
28 x 36 in.
Reference: Egerton 1978,
306–8 (no. 331)

JOHN WILLIS GOOD

Before the Race
and *After the Race,*
c.1872–3

Bronze, heights 12 3/4 in.
and 10 3/4 in. respectively

ADRIAN JONES

Horse and stable-lad, c.1890

Bronze, height 13 3/4 in.

JOSEPH EDGAR BOEHM

St. Simon, 1885

Bronze, height 22 1/4 in.

ADRIAN JONES

The Tetrarch, c.1890

Bronze, height 23 in.

JOHN LAVERY

Jockeys and owners at Epsom, c.1920

Oil on panel, 20 x 24 in.

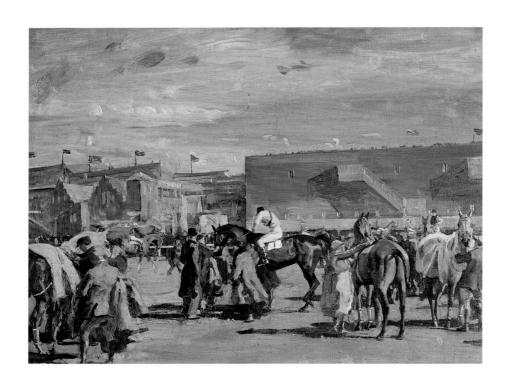

ALFRED MUNNINGS

*Saddling Up
for the Grand National, 1919:
Before the Snowstorm (sketch)*, 1919

Oil on canvas, 21 1/2 x 29 3/4 in.

ALFRED MUNNINGS

The Saddling Paddock, Cheltenham March Meeting (sketch), c.1947

Oil on panel, 16 3/4 x 27 1/2 in.
Possibly exhibited at the Royal Academy, London, 1947

ALFRED MUNNINGS

Saddling Up
for the Grand National, 1919:
Before the Snowstorm, 1919

Oil on canvas, 40 x 50 in.
Exhibited at the Royal Academy,
London, 1928

The Grand National, run at Aintree outside Liverpool, is the most prestigious British steeplechasing event. In 1919 the winner was the favorite, Poethlyn, shown here in the center of the composition. Paul Mellon admired Alfred Munnings as the modern successor to the great sporting artists of the eighteenth and early nineteenth centuries, and his favorite portrait of himself was the one Munnings painted in 1936 (page 13). He bought SADDLING UP FOR THE GRAND NATIONAL *and its preparatory sketch (page 98) at opposite ends of his collecting career, the sketch in 1954 and the large picture in 1989. They hung with fifteen other paintings by Munnings, as well as a number of drawings, in the conference room at his New York office.*

ALFRED MUNNINGS

Hyperion, 1937

Oil on canvas,
19 3/8 x 23 1/2 in.

*Hyperion was a highly successful
horse bred and owned by the
Earl of Derby; he was foaled in
1930, by Gainsborough out of
Selene. In 1933 he was
unbeaten, winning the Derby,
the St. Leger, the Chester Vase,
and the Prince of Wales Stakes
at Ascot. From 1935 he was at
Lord Derby's stud at Newmarket,
where Munnings painted him
in his loose-box. He sired many
famous racehorses, and was
an ancestor of Paul Mellon's
Mill Reef.*

ALFRED MUNNINGS

*John Hay Whitney's Royal Minstrel,
with Joe Childs up*, c.1929

Oil on canvas, 12 x 16 in.

ALFRED MUNNINGS

Southern Hero and Black Speck, the property of J. V. Rank, 1940

Oil on board, 17 3/4 x 24 in.

ALFRED MUNNINGS

Newmarket Again, 1950s

Oil on panel, 17 3/4 x 24 in. Exhibited at the Royal Academy, London, 1958

JOHN SKEAPING

Racing group, 1977

Artist's proof
Bronze, height 11 7/8 in.

JOHN SKEAPING

Mares and Foals, 1978

From the edition of 10
Bronze, height 12 1/2 in.

Paul Mellon's favorite sporting artist of his own generation was the sculptor John Skeaping. Among the many Skeapings he acquired, the RACING GROUP, *showing five racehorses in a tight finish, was one of the most elaborate; the others included studies of both horses and dogs, especially greyhounds. Given his interest in the tradition of racehorse portraiture, Paul Mellon commissioned few portraits of his own horses; in almost every case his chosen artist was Skeaping, who in 1972 made a half-life-size bronze of the great Mill Reef.*

JOHN SKEAPING

Greyhound, c.1978

Artist's proof
Bronze, height 34 in.

JOHN SKEAPING

Double Form, c.1970

Artist's proof
Bronze, height 20 1/2 in.

The Working Horse

"There are so many ways to look at horses. To some of us the living horse is a work of art. Even the structure of the skeleton, the bones, as depicted by George Stubbs in his ANATOMY OF THE HORSE, *give us a fair comprehension of the easy motion, the force of propulsion rising into speed, the interaction and integration of many separate and sometimes minute parts which comprise the horse in action. The plough horse straining at the traces with powerful stride and deliberate rhythm, the Hackney trotting with light step and alert head, the polo pony jinking and swerving like an athlete, the hunter or 'chaser gliding easily over a great fence, the Thoroughbred with his ears pricked, galloping gracefully down to the starting stalls, all form pictures in our minds which have much the same attributes as fine paintings or drawings."*

—Paul Mellon, 1980 [1]

The Paul Mellon bequest represents every aspect of the life of the horse within human society, not only hunting and racing, but also the more mundane tasks of pulling carts, coaches, carriages, and ploughs, and the sometimes harsh realities of being bought and sold in the marketplace. The early nineteenth century saw the rise of a distinct new genre of sporting art, the coaching scene, with James Pollard as its most successful exponent. The Pollards collected by Paul Mellon show the splendor of the coaching age while also giving a sense of its inevitable demise. By the early Victorian period, as the horsedrawn mail- or stage-coach gave way to the railroad train, the sight of a jaunty, handsomely decorated coach was already becoming the stuff of nostalgia. As far as the horse as provider of power was concerned, Pollard's paintings of a Royal Mail ignominiously loaded onto a train and *The Last of the Mail Coaches at Newcastle upon Tyne* (pages 112–13) show the beginning of the end.

The same valedictory spirit pervades the work of the early twentieth–century painter Robert Bevan. With a remarkable blend of realism and sympathy, Bevan described the plight of individual horses, overburdened and sold into lower and tougher forms of work, and at the same time suggested the coming redundancy of working horses as a class. His scenes from the lives of London horses take on a special poignancy when viewed against the background of the rise of motor transport, which completed the replacement of the working horse by the machine. Whereas Paul Mellon's enthusiasm for earlier artists such as Stubbs and Constable has been widely known for many years, his admiration for Bevan is one of the revelations of his bequest: it contains nine Bevan paintings and a number of drawings and prints.

1. Baskett 1980, foreword, 7–8.

GEORGE STUBBS

Labourers, 1781

Enamel, on Wedgwood biscuit
earthenware, oval, 27 1/2 x 36 in.
Reference: Egerton, 1984, 77 (no. 48)

Stubbs worked closely with the famous master potter Josiah Wedgwood to develop ceramic tablets on which to paint in enamel. Here the design is based on an earlier oil painting showing servants of George, Viscount Torrington, laying bricks on his estate, Southill in Bedfordshire. The building to the right is a new lodge presumably built by these same men. According to the artist's early biographer Ozias Humphry, he had been watching them at work for some time when they fell into a dispute about the right way of replacing the tailboard on the cart, and this was the moment he chose to depict. The painting was bought from Stubbs by Wedgwood and remained in the Wedgwood family until bought at auction by Paul Mellon in 1978.

JOHN CONSTABLE

Horses and cart, 1814

Oil on canvas laid on board, 6 3/8 x 10 1/2 in.
Reference: Reynolds 1996, 199 (no. 14.40)

JAMES POLLARD

Schooling a pair in a brake at Lucas's Repository, Clerkenwell, 1818

Oil on canvas, 17 x 13 in.

References: Selway 1972, 23 (no. 1); Egerton 1978, 267–8 (no. 292)

JOHN FERNELEY

*William Massey-Stanley
driving his cabriolet
in Hyde Park,*
1833

Oil on canvas
43 1/2 x 62 1/2 in.
Reference: Egerton 1978,
246–7 (no. 266)

JACQUES–LAURENT
AGASSE

Old Smithfield Market,
1824

Oil on canvas
20 x 27 1/2 in.

JAMES POLLARD

John Smith Barry's private drag and grey team, 1824

Oil on canvas, 32 x 48 in.
References: Taylor 1964, 80 (no. 284);
Selway 1972, 24 (no. 13);
Egerton 1978, 270–1 (no. 295)

John Smith Barry, of Marbury Hall, Cheshire, was a devotee of the sport of driving and a keen member of the driving club founded by his cousin the Earl of Barrymore; it was known variously as the Whip Club, the Four in Hand Club, and the Barouche Driving Club. The members prided themselves not only on their skills as drivers but also on a splendid appearance. This is evident in Pollard's painting of the coachyard at Marbury: the black and yellow drag, the grooms in livery of the same colors, and the team of grey horses are all impeccably turned out.

JAMES POLLARD

*The London-Faringdon
Stage Coach
passing Buckland House,
Berkshire,* 1835

Oil on canvas,
19 7/8 x 27 5/8 in.
References: Selway 1972, 29
(no. 91); Egerton 1978,
275–6 (no. 300)

JOHN FREDERICK
HERRING, SR.

*Grey carriage horses in the
coachyard at Putteridge Bury,
Hertfordshire,* 1838

Oil on canvas
40 1/8 x 50 1/8 in.
Reference: Egerton 1978,
303–4 (no. 327)

JAMES POLLARD

The London–Manchester Stage Coach, the "Peveril of the Peak," outside the Peacock Inn, Islington, 1835

Oil on canvas, 13 1/2 x 17 1/2 in.
References: Taylor 1963, 190 (no. 363); Selway 1972, 29 (no. 90); Egerton 1978, 276 (no. 301)

JAMES POLLARD

The Louth–London Royal Mail loaded onto a train at Peterborough East, Northamptonshire, 1845

Oil on canvas, 9 1/4 x 12 1/8 in.
References: Selway 1972, 31 (no. 127); Egerton 1978, 279–80 (no. 305)

JAMES POLLARD >

The Last of the Mail Coaches at Newcastle upon Tyne, 1848

Oil on canvas, 18 x 27 in.
References: Taylor 1963, 191 (no. 365); Selway 1972, 32 (no. 139); Egerton 1978, 280–1 (no. 306)

The lid and front of this decorated cigar box show the Taglioni Coach, which was a private vehicle owned jointly by the Earl of Chesterfield and Count Batthyany, both members of the Richmond Driving Club. The coach took its name from Marie Taglioni, the most celebrated ballet dancer of the time; its door panel was painted with a portrait of her in LA SYLPHIDE. The decorations were copied from popular prints after James Pollard and Charles Cooper Henderson respectively. The sides and back of the box, also based on prints, show Taglioni, another dancer named Pauline Duvernay, and a hunting scene.

ARTIST UNKNOWN
The Taglioni Coach and other scenes, c.1840

Oil, on a wooden cigar box, height 5 3/8 in.
Reference: Egerton 1978, 282 (no. 307)

Pollard shows the arrival of the Edinburgh-London Royal Mail coach in Newcastle for the last time on 5 July 1847, having been superseded by the railroad. To mark the sad occasion the coachman and guard wore black mourning bands in their hats and flew the Union flag at half mast, surmounted by a banner of black crêpe. "It was impossible to record the death of the mail coach without regret," reported the NEWCASTLE JOURNAL, "for it really was a noble establishment, and not many years ago was looked upon as one of the glories of the country, of which the public had just cause to be proud. But, it is gone, after a reign of not more than sixty-one years . . . The horses of the various contractors of the line are announced for sale by auction."[1] Pollard painted the scene for his friend and patron Edward Macnamara, who at this time was the sole contractor for the distribution of the mail— by horse and cart— within London.

1. 10 July 1847, quoted in Egerton 1978, 281.

ROBERT BEVAN

The Turn-Rice Plough, Sussex

c.1909–10

Oil on canvas,
26 1/8 x 35 1/2 in.
Exhibited
at the Allied Artists'
Association, London,
1910
Reference: Bevan 1965
(no. 23)

ALFRED MUNNINGS

*Horse fair
in East Anglia*

1899

Watercolor,
13 1/2 x 20 in.

114

ROBERT BEVAN
Ploughing team
c.1905–6

Black crayon, 8 1/2 x 11 in.

ROBERT BEVAN
Timber hauling, c.1917

Crayon, 13 11/16 x 17 in.

HERBERT HASELTINE

Left: *Harboro' Nulli Secundus, Shire Stallion,*
from the *British Champion Animals* series,
modeled 1921–2

Posthumous cast, 1968
Bronze, height 14 1/2 in.
Reference: Cormack 1996, 18–21

Right: *Sudborne Premier, Suffolk Punch Stallion,*
from the *British Champion Animals* series,
modeled 1922

Posthumous cast, 1964–5
Bronze, height 12 1/4 in.
Reference: Cormack 1996, 22–9

ALFRED MUNNINGS

Royal Grey
in State Harness,
c.1925

Oil on millboard,
13 1/4 x 16 in.

HERBERT HASELTINE

Splendour, Queen
Alexandra's carriage
horse, 1910

From the edition of 2
Bronze, height 17 in.

ROBERT BEVAN

"Quiet with all road nuisances"
c.1912

Exhibited at the Carfax Gallery,
London, 1912
Oil on canvas, 19 1/8 x 24 1/4 in.
References: Bevan 1965 (no. 37);
Baron and Cormack 1980, 2–4 (no. 2)

*Bevan sketched and painted at various London horse markets, in this case
Aldridge's on Upper St. Martin's Lane, near Leicester Square. The title of the
work comes from the auctioneer's description of the horse for sale: supposedly
untroubled by the noises of the street, especially modern motor traffic, it will make
a good horse for urban use, probably pulling a cab or delivery van. Its hunter clip,
with the saddle area of its coat left longer than the rest, is the reminder of a
former life in the country.*

ROBERT BEVAN

The Horse Mart
(sketch)

c.1917

Crayon,
9 1/4 x 13 in.
Reference: Baron
and Cormack
1980, 8 (no. 13)

ROBERT BEVAN

The Horse Mart

c.1917–18

Oil on canvas, 20 x 28 in.
References: Bevan 1965
(no. 64); Baron and
Cormack 1980,
8–9 (no. 12)

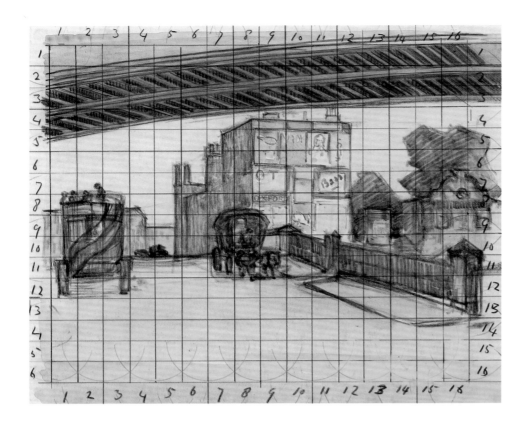

ROBERT BEVAN

Two Bridges, 1912–13

Crayon and watercolor, squared for transfer,
10 1/4 x 12 1/2 in.

ROBERT BEVAN

The Weigh House,
Cumberland Market,
c.1914

Oil on canvas,
20 1/8 x 24 1/8 in.

Bevan lived in the north
London suburb of Hampstead but
in 1914 took a studio overlook-
ing the Cumberland hay and
straw market in town. From
his second-floor window he
painted different views of the
market square, here the north
side with the weigh house in
the center. In them the place of
business looks empty and
slightly forlorn, hinting at the
decline of the equine economy
of which it was a center.

ROBERT BEVAN

Hay Carts, Cumberland Market (sketch), c.1915

Crayon, squared
for transfer, 10 1/4 x 13 in.

ROBERT BEVAN

Hay Carts, Cumberland Market, 1915

Oil on canvas,
18 7/8 x 24 in.
References:
Bevan 1965 (no. 49)
Baron and Cormack
1980, 6–7 (no. 9)

ROBERT BEVAN

The Bayhorse, Tattersall's (design for a London Underground poster), 1921

Crayon and chalk, 13 1/2 x 11 1/2 in.
Reference: Bevan 1965 (no. 74)

ROBERT BEVAN

A Morning at Tattersall's, 1921

Oil on canvas, 25 1/8 x 30 1/8 in.
Reference: Baron and Cormack 1980,
10−11 (no. 16)

As the presence of the finely dressed people on the left suggests, Tattersall's was the upmarket London auction house for horses, handling the sale of racehorses, hunters, and gentlemen's carriage horses. The firm was founded in the eighteenth century. When painted by James Pollard in the 1830s (page 91), it was still in its original premises at Hyde Park Corner; by Bevan's time it had moved to the Albert Gate, Knightsbridge, taking with it the statue of a fox under a cupola that had become its trademark. Bevan was a familiar sight at the horse auctions. His son recalled that he always looked at home there, and "rather relished looking like a man who had more to do with horses and hounds than with canvas and paint." [1]

1. Bevan 1965, 20.

ROBERT BEVAN

Crocks, c.1924

Crayon, 11 x 13 1/2 in.
Reference: Baron and Cormack 1980,
10–11 (no. 17)

Bibliography

Works are listed in chronological order by date
of publication.

Basil Taylor, *Sport and the Horse*, exhibition catalogue,
foreword by Leslie Cheek, Virginia Museum of Fine
Arts, Richmond, 1960

Basil Taylor, *Painting in England 1700–1850.
Collection of Mr and Mrs Paul Mellon*, exhibition
catalogue, foreword by Leslie Cheek, Virginia
Museum of Fine Arts, Richmond, 1963

Paul Mellon, *A Collector Recollects. Remarks by Paul
Mellon at the Opening of the Exhibition "Painting in
England 1700–1850,"* Virginia Museum of Fine Arts,
Richmond, 1963 (reprinted in part in Yale Center for
British Art 1977, v–ix)

Basil Taylor, *Painting in England 1700–1850 from
the Collection of Mr and Mrs Paul Mellon*, exhibition
catalogue, Royal Academy of Arts, London, 1964
(version of Taylor 1963)

R. A. Bevan, *Robert Bevan 1865–1925. A memoir by
his son*, London, 1965

Basil Taylor, *Stubbs*, London, 1971

N. C. Selway, *The Golden Age of Coaching and Sport
As Depicted by James Pollard*, Leigh-on-Sea, 1972

Yale Center for British Art, *Selected Paintings,
Drawings, and Books*, New Haven, 1977

Judy Egerton, *Sport in Art and Books. The Paul Mellon
Collection: British Sporting and Animal Paintings
1655–1867*, Tate Gallery, London, for the Yale Center
for British Art, 1978

Judy Egerton and Dudley Snelgrove, *Sport in Art and
Books. The Paul Mellon Collection: British Sporting and
Animal Drawings c. 1500–1850*, Tate Gallery, London,
for the Yale Center for British Art, 1978

Aubrey Noakes, *Ben Marshall 1768–1835*,
Leigh-on-Sea, 1978

Wendy Baron and Malcolm Cormack, *The Camden
Town Group*, exhibition catalogue, Yale Center for
British Art, New Haven, 1980

John Baskett, *The Horse in Art*, foreword by Paul
Mellon, Boston, 1980

Ellen D'Oench, *The Conversation Piece: Arthur Devis
and his Contemporaries*, exhibition catalogue, Yale
Center for British Art, New Haven, 1980

John B. Podeschi, *Sport in Art and Books. The Paul
Mellon Collection: Books on the Horse and Horsemanship.
Riding, Hunting, Breeding and Racing 1400–1941*,
Tate Gallery, London, for the Yale Center for British
Art, 1981

Judy Egerton, *George Stubbs 1724–1806*, exhibition
catalogue, Tate Gallery, London, and Yale Center
for British Art, New Haven, 1984

Graham Reynolds, *The Later Paintings and Drawings
of John Constable*, 2 vols, published for the Paul Mellon
Centre for Studies in British Art, New Haven and
London, 1984

Helmut von Erffa and Allen Staley, *The Paintings of
Benjamin West*, New Haven and London, 1986

John Wilmerding, ed., *Essays in Honor of Paul Mellon, Collector and Benefactor*, National Gallery of Art, Washington, 1986

Herbert S. Bailey, Jr., et al., *In Praise of Paul Mellon*, privately printed, 1987

Paul Mellon, with John Baskett, *Reflections in a Silver Spoon: A Memoir*, New York, 1992

Malcolm Cormack, *Champion Animals. Sculptures by Herbert Haseltine*, Virginia Museum of Fine Arts, Richmond, 1996

Graham Reynolds, *The Early Paintings and Drawings of John Constable*, 2 vols, published for the Paul Mellon Centre for Studies in British Art, New Haven and London, 1996

Patrick McCaughey, "Paul Mellon and the British Imagination," *This Other Eden. Paintings from the Yale Center for British Art*, New Haven and London, 1998, 1–21

Index of Artists

JOHN BASKETT was a close friend and advisor to Paul Mellon,
with whom he collaborated on a memoir,
Reflections in a Silver Spoon (1992).

MALCOLM WARNER is Senior Curator of Paintings and Sculpture
at the Yale Center for British Art.